Reading Begins at Home

Dorothy Butler is internationally recognised as an authority on children's books and reading. With a degree in English and a Diploma in Education, she taught before founding and running her Children's Bookshop and a Reading Centre for children with reading difficulties. She has worked as a consulting editor, taught children's literature for the University of Auckland, conducted writing courses, and written her own books. Prominent among her books for adults are *Cushla and Her Books* and *Babies Need Books*.

Photo courtesy of Reading Recovery Council of North America

Marie Clay, Emeritus Professor, taught in primary schools, studied Developmental Psychology at the University of Minnesota on a Fulbright scholarship, completed her doctorate on 'Emergent Literacy' and devoted her academic and working life to understanding early reading development. Her work has influenced the lives of millions of children across the world.

Reading Begins at Home

Preparing children for reading before they go to school

The authors wish to thank Brenda Marshall for the illustrations and cover design,
and Professor Mary Anne Doyle of the University of Connecticut for her reading of the text.
The help of Frances Plumpton in compiling the booklist in Chapter Six is also
acknowledged with gratitude.

Reprinted 2008, 2015

Global Education Systems [GES] Ltd
132A St Stephens Avenue, Parnell, Auckland 1052, New Zealand

ISBN NZ 978-1-86970-601-2
ISBN USA 978-0-325-01714-3
ISBN UK 978-1-40716006-1

Distributed by
Australia: Scholastic Australia Pty Ltd, PO Box 579, Gosford, NSW 2250
ABN 11 000 614 577
www.scholastic.com.au

New Zealand: Scholastic New Zealand Ltd, Private Bag 94407, Botany, Auckland 2163
www.scholastic.co.nz

UK and Eire: Scholastic Ltd, Book End, Range Road, Witney, Oxfordshire OX29 0YD
www.scholastic.co.uk/marieclay

United States: Heinemann, 361 Hanover Street, Portsmouth, NH 03801-3912
www.heinemann.com

Library of Congress Cataloging-in-Publication Data
Butler, Dorothy, 1925-
Reading begins at home : preparing children for reading before they go
to school / Dorothy Butler with Marie Clay. -- 2nd ed. p. cm.
1. Children--Books and reading. 2. Reading readiness. 3.
Reading--Parent participation. I. Clay, Marie M. II. Title.
Z1037.A1B88 2008
028.5'5--dc22
2007048642

Printed in China by Nordica

Contents

Something to think about
one

There was a time when no one even thought about teaching their children to read before they went to school. School was the place for children to start learning to read. Everyone knew that.

These days, many parents are not so sure. They wonder whether their children will become better readers if they are taught earlier. As children don't go to school until they are five or six or seven in some countries, should parents intervene? How soon? Two, three, four ...? Would this mean that reading failure – today's bogey – could be avoided?

What do we mean by 'reading'?

If we are going to get involved in the issue, we need to be clear what reading *is*. (We will ignore the little boy who said it was 'talk writ down', though I acknowledge his insight with humble respect.)

The best definition I know is this: 'Reading is the transfer of meaning from one mind to another through the medium of written language.'

This, of course, does not tell us how either of these minds works to accomplish the wonder.

Let's concentrate on the mind which is *receiving* the message; that is, the mind of the *reader*. How does that person's mind process the 'written language' to receive the message?

It may be useful at this point to think of the way in which the child learns to speak. No one actually teaches children to speak, and yet, by three or four years of age, they have learned to produce the right sounds, organised in an extremely complex way, to express an almost infinite number of ideas.

Children do this expertly, without direct help from adults. Children are not just mimics.

They create sentences to express their thoughts. It is surely sensible to look closely at the method they use. What units of speech do they produce first?

You may say that the baby first says sounds and then single words. But anyone who has handled an 18-month-old will know that when the child says 'ball' this means a great deal more than a name for a toy. He or she may be making one of many possible statements: *'There's my ball'* with a pleased smile, on finding it; *'My ball has run away down the hill!'* with outstretched arm and concerned expression; *'No! I don't want to go to bed! I want to play with my ball!'* struggling desperately as a parent lowers the child into the cot!

All these meanings and many more can be understood when this child uses the one word 'ball'. We are meant to understand the rest of the sentence because the child cannot say it. There is no doubt that the child has the meaning in his or her mind.

How does this relate to reading?

There is nothing simple about the way small childern learn to speak; and there is nothing simple about how they learn to read. But they have to *learn*; the process must take place in their *minds*, regardless of what the adult out there does. In fact, I would say it is impossible to 'teach' anyone to read. We must help them to learn. Isn't it sensible, then, to think about *how* they learn?

Before continuing, there is one factor about learning to read which should be remembered, and always considered. Learning requires *effort*, and the effort must be seen as worthwhile by the learner. It also requires *practice* to become a fluent reader, and the hours required could never be provided in the school day. The practice must take place at home. It is fair to ask: In how many homes is so much effortless, mindless entertainment provided by electronic equipment that the child is discouraged – prevented, in many cases – from discovering the rewards from books?

In the days when I was involved in helping children to acquire or increase reading skills, I commonly found 11- and 12-year-olds who had mastered essential skills in the early days at school and, quite simply, never bothered to practise them since! When it comes to the point, reading has much in common with swimming, tennis and many other sports, arts and crafts. The only way to become proficient is to practise; once you have, with practice, achieved a certain competence, satisfaction and then pleasure in the pursuit follows. And so it is with reading.

How should we 'teach' (or help children to learn) to read?

It is usual to break tasks into their separate parts when teaching a new skill, finally combining the parts. It seems reasonable, perhaps, to approach reading in this way.

- Teach the children the sounds of the 26 letters in the alphabet.
- Teach them to assemble these letters into words.
- Teach them to combine these words into sentences.

Task accomplished. But is it?

During my days in remedial reading, I constantly found that many nine- and 10-year-olds who came to me knew the sounds of the letters, and could recognise them. Most of them believed that sounding out words one after the other was 'what reading was'. Their reading was, as a result, a stumbling affair. Children would be stuck on a word, without any idea that looking back, or forward, or thinking about it would help them to get the message – and quite likely, then, to realise what the word was, and remember it.

Once the 'single word' habit is ingrained, it is *very* hard to overcome; and being 'stuck on a word' with only 'sounding out' to help means that you have lost track of the meaning of the sentence.

There is considerable evidence that the majority of failed readers see reading in this way, and not as 'getting the message'. On the other hand, young children who are becoming good readers can often be seen to be almost swallowing the print whole, keeping the sense going by a miraculous mobilisation of all the resources at their disposal – an exhilarating experience!

This seems to suggest that paying attention to 'the message' is a helpful idea. Actually, children have to master this sooner or later, regardless of how they start.

But surely letters and words are important

Of course they are! It would be ludicrous to suggest that language could be written down without letters and words. They are the vital components of reading. But this does not mean that they should be learned in isolation. Experience shows that learning letters and words takes place best while the child is working with whole messages.

What about phonics?

By phonics you probably mean beginning with simple words like 'cat' and 'mat', and showing children how to 'sound them out' letter by letter. Then you probably make a sentence: 'The cat sat on the mat.' Even here, if you want children to sound out each word you run into trouble. 'The' does not obey the rules. You are obliged to tell the children what 'the' says, and hope for the best.

Either you ignore their possible confusion (after all, you have just told them it is possible to sound words out), or you tell them that 'the' is an exception, and five-year-olds are not strong on exceptions. Before long, they meet other ordinary words which also flout the rules: 'mother', 'water', 'through', 'love', 'many', 'could', 'friend', 'want' ... The trouble is that English has 26 letters but 44 sounds, many of which are made by a combination of letters that is not consistent from word to word. They're not going to get there with phonics alone.

Of course the letters help; they are vital to reading and writing. I like to talk about 'sensible use of the alphabet', recognising that 'knowing your sounds' helps often – particularly noting the first and last letters of a word. But this is just one of the clues children need for the reading game. Well-prepared children use their imaginations, their knowledge of language and how it works, their familiarity with letters and words – and get the message. Trying to limp along on sounds alone simply doesn't get you there.

You may be confused by this talk about learning letters and words in 'messages' instead of on charts or word cards. This is understandable; the reading process *is* complex, not simple. Surely, working with what research has shown must occur in the child's mind is the sensible, reliable way to go. You need not worry about this; but it may be useful to listen to a 'cautionary tale' about what will *not* be useful, and may even be harmful when school starts.

> An interesting illustration of how one kind of learning can block another kind of learning from happening was reported recently. The mother concerned taught her little boy to recognise 300 words before he went to school. That was an unusually large list and they must have worked as a wonderful teaching-learning team. After he had been at school for a year the mother went to discuss his lack of progress with the teacher. The mother could not understand why he was not moving more rapidly through the school programme. The teacher asked the boy to read one of the earliest and simplest reading books. On continuous text in the story-book, he could not read. He had the wrong idea about reading. He thought he was supposed to find that word 'in his head' from his 300 words, and say it. He did not understand that all the skills he had for speaking could help him anticipate words following one another in the story. He did not know that the plot could also guide him, and that the letters could give him clues. For him reading was flash recognition of a snapshot view of a word. This can be a starting point for some children, who are quick to find out there are other ways of getting to accurate reading. But this little boy was so good at word recognition, and he had practised it so well for so long, that his first reaction was to 'word call' and he found it very difficult to understand and then remember that reading involves many other things. Even when he remembered, he found it difficult to be flexible, because well-established habits have a way of controlling us.

This story demonstrates very well, of course, that words are best learned in sentences. Flashing word cards at children can defeat the purpose of real reading.

A word of reassurance

If you have found any of the foregoing material a bit difficult to understand, don't worry. Read the suggestions in the following sections, and try them out. And if you are among those parents who have always cuddled their babies, talked to them, sung to them, chanted the old remembered nursery rhymes, played 'This little piggy' and 'Round and round the garden' … you will have made a good start anyway.

Back to the under-fives: what can parents do?

The days from birth to school entry are vitally important; these are the days when the children's minds are developing rapidly, and should be nourished with conversation, stories read aloud and told, songs sung and games played. None of this should happen in a 'teacherly' way; a background of loving security, with laughter, play and shared interests, as the children's perception of the world and their role in it widens, is the best possible preparation for school – and life.

And of course, an important ingredient of this ideal life will be a start on the road to *writing*.

One of the most helpful things parents can do for their children is to provide them from earliest days with paper, crayons, pencils – later, safe felt-tip markers – and a place to use them, such as the kitchen table. Children sometimes come to school quite unprepared to sit at a table and do *anything*. These children have not learned to concentrate on any sort of bookish activity, and must somehow be given experiences that try to compensate – an almost impossible task, in many cases.

Writing really *does* go hand in hand with reading. Fortunate children are well on the way towards both skills. By school entry, they will have been provided with suitable materials, and have started to scribble cheerfully before they are two. By the time they come to school, they are turning out pictures of (usually) recognisable people, houses, cars, trees and all the features of their lives, and are often able to write their own names, or at least their initial.

Such children have confidence in their own ability to learn, and this is an enormous advantage; and they know they can communicate in other ways than talking. When children bring us a picture that they have just done, we *know* they mean this as a communication, as well as a token of affection.

Some children invent writing (scribbling), the meaning of which they will tell you if asked.

> By the time Anthony went to school, he was filling whole pages of lined paper with neat 'writing', always keeping to the lines, and starting on the left side. After he had been at school for about a month he said to his mother,
>
> *'Mrs Smith wants me to stop doing my writing and start doing hers.'*
>
> *'What do you think?'* his mother asked.
>
> *'I don't know,'* he said uncertainly. *'I can say better things in mine!'*

Once he decided to change to 'Mrs Smith's writing', he just *had* to make it say the things he wanted.

At home
two

Ideas about reading are more readily caught than taught in the very early years. Children who grow up in families where people read will come to feel that books and papers are worth attention. They certainly take attention away from them! Perhaps they will try to 'get into the scene' by crawling into Dad's lap, putting themselves between the paper and their father.

A great deal of research has gone into the problem of why some children seem to learn quickly and easily at school, and others make little progress. Here are the conclusions:

- In their children's education, parents are in the middle of the stage.
- The sort of home a child comes from, and in particular whether or not it contains books, is of vital importance.
- Where strong parental interest links up with the presence of books, children forge ahead.

The theme that runs through the research is that homes are more effective in producing readers than the kind of schools children attend; and the research does not identify the *wealthiest* homes as the most successful. The presence of books, and adults who share them with their children, belong to libraries, visit bookshops and behave as if books *matter* – these are the things that make the difference, in homes of any income level.

All of these investigations were undertaken with the intention of discovering those factors which contribute to children's progress in learning to read. The evidence showed overwhelmingly that parents matter.

What does all this mean in positive terms? It means that from the earliest days parents, in our kind of society, should introduce their children to the world of books. They should read to them often and they should look closely at themselves as readers. They present a vital example for their children to copy.

Parents as readers

Does your child see you reading books, as well as newspapers and magazines? Children in many modern homes may never see an adult concentrating for any considerable period of time on anything except the television screen or computer.

Pages of print can look forbidding to children who cannot read. On the other hand, if children see their parents utterly absorbed in a book, they are likely to feel that such an experience is worth striving towards.

> A five-year-old girl once snatched such a book from her father and, her eyes fixed with frustration on the incomprehensible text, said with some passion: *'Tell me what's in it! Read it to me!'* She was certain it must be fascinating. Dad hadn't taken his eyes off it for the last hour!

Writing: true partner to reading

If watching parents and others use books as part of everyday life helps a child to become a reader, so sharing in family activities which involve print has its role. The capacity of print to capture human speech is fascinating.

Certainly, many people today send emails instead of writing letters or cards, but there are still, mercifully, some people who send real letters. In most families there are, from time to time, birthday invitations to send out, thank you letters to write, telephone messages to record, and the all-important grocery list to make. There are still pens, pencils and paper in the average home, and watching adults use them and experimenting oneself is a powerful learning process for children. The idea that messages can come from marks on the page that other people have made with pen or pencil encourages children to try their skill at both 'getting' and 'sending' messages. This is one of the ways in which they start to learn about letters and words, as they need them, for their own purposes.

It is not only in the field of reading and writing that the child will be forging ahead in such a family. From earliest days, thoughtful parents can involve their child in learning that just seems to happen; learning that is fun.

Finding opportunities

Think of the learning points in the following exchanges, remembering that the mother might easily have said, *'Run away now, I want to read my letter.'*

'Look, Tessa, a letter from Grandpa! Let's see what he says.' Almost certainly, Grandpa has written on the bottom 'Love to Tessa' and this can be pointed out, examined and savoured.

Let's consider Grandpa's letter:

- People can 'talk' in one place and by writing their 'talking' onto paper make sure that another person 'hears' later.
- People who are fond of one another keep in touch by doing this. Both enjoy it.
- It is usual to answer a letter. Sometimes, a particular question needs an answer. Sometimes, you just chat.

Or: *'I'm just writing a list of what we need at the supermarket. Can you think of anything?'* The hopeful response may well be *'Chocolate biscuits!'* or *'Ice cream!'* but drawing the child's attention to the humble grocery list is just another way of illustrating that writing thoughts down to be used later is part of life – as are diaries and calendars, which in most homes are used for marking ordinary things like dentist appointments as well as exciting things like birthdays.

Even showing the small child the electricity bill, with, *'We'll have to write a cheque and post it'* and a casual word about what electricity is used for in the house, puts the child in the picture. (Even if you use computer banking you are sure to have to post a cheque for something, sometime.)

From such experience, there will be a constant flow of information about envelopes, stamps, postcards, not to mention the growth of confidence which comes from knowing, progressively, how things work. The real point is that all this learning can proceed easily, gradually and inevitably if parents get into the habit of involving their children in the ordinary things of life; and, for the particular purpose of this book, the child's attention will be constantly directed at letters and words in their right and proper place, as part of messages conveyed from one human mind to another.

What about money and time that parents may not have?

Many parents of young children think that helping them to learn will require materials that they can't afford, or time that they don't have. This is not true at all: opportunities are there in any family on the dullest day, with no special equipment. You must have noticed how the youngest children can't keep their hands off papers, objects, books and pens that are lying around. All too often this tremendous urge to inspect, to handle, to manipulate is attributed to sheer naughtiness, which of course it's not. If adults take the trouble to 'help' with this endless investigation into the fascinating ways of the world, the learning that takes place will be considerable. The youngster will learn to look closely, to handle carefully, to listen intently.

Back to family letters. Children love to receive letters of their own, long before they can read or write, and this is one way in which grandparents and others can help. 'Answering' the letter is fun and sometimes produces an astonishing result.

> Sophie, aged four, and her older sister and brother had received books as presents from a relative. The older children were writing thank you notes, and suggested that Sophie draw a picture to go in the envelope. Sophie clearly felt unattracted to this idea. She found a sheet of lined paper. *'Write "Dear Aunty Jean",'* she instructed her mother.

> This being done, she filled the page with 'writing', line after line, always starting at the left margin, keeping to the lines and using a neat, regular 'script' which bore an astonishing resemblance to 'real writing'. Near the bottom, she stopped. *'Now write "Love from Sophie",'* she requested, adding a shaky S of her own.

Think how much this little girl knew already about letter writing:

- Letters begin at the top with 'Dear …' (the person with whom you wish to communicate).
- Letters end at the bottom with 'Love from …' (the person who is writing).
- Written language proceeds from left to right across the page, and from the top to the bottom of the page.
- Lines on note paper are there to help you keep your writing neat and orderly.

There was no doubt in Sophie's mind that Aunty Jean would be pleased to receive her letter, and none in ours that Sophie was well on her way to mastering the business of turning speech into written symbols and getting it back again. That is, she was learning to read.

Alphabet letters

From an early age children love knowing and identifying their own first initial and will practise writing it, often in strange or inappropriate places: Diana raised a laugh in her family some years ago.

> Diana's mother was annoyed one day to find a bold if wobbly 'D' on the back of the sofa.
>
> Mother (not very pleased): *'Who wrote "D" on the back of the sofa?'*
> Diana: *'In green crayon?'*
> Mother (surprised): *'Yes …'*
> Diana (firmly): *'Not me!'*

Once they recognise their own first initial of course, children seem to find it everywhere.

> Jack, aged four, came home from kindergarten with a large 'J', which he had written himself, on his painting. His three-year-old brother, Ben, requested his 'letter' and was quite fascinated with the large 'B' his mother wrote for him. Later he was seen to be crouched on the floor in the kitchen, his face against the boards, peering at a tiny engraved plate at the base of the refrigerator. Suddenly, in a muffled but triumphant voice he said, *'It's only got one Jack, but it's got two Bennies!'*

Alphabet friezes which may be mounted or pinned up on the wall (low enough for the children to see them) are both attractive and useful for letter recognition. There are usually several clear and colourful versions on the market. Curiosity and learning can be stimulated by these, but a word of caution is not out of place.

Singing or saying the alphabet is fun, and children usually learn this skill before school.

This does not mean, however, that they have learned to recognise each letter, and it can lead to confusion. An over-emphasis on letter *names* can make the learning of letter *sounds* difficult, for example.

Of course, for some purposes in the future (dictionaries and phone books, for example) the child will need to know the *order* of the letters in the alphabet, so there is no need to worry. But try to be flexible. Point out individual letters to your child as the opportunity crops up.

Children can make lots of discoveries with a package of plastic letters which have little magnets set into them. Using a steel oven tray they can sort and arrange the ones they like best. Slowly, bit by bit, they will add to the groups of letters they know. A few favourite words can be learned in this way. Magnetic letters can be used in many different ways and, unlike an alphabet frieze, they can be put down and taken apart. These activities appeal to young children. Keep a tray of magnetic letters near the fridge. Smallest family members enjoy 'writing' their names on the fridge door.

Some children seem to love symbols and, once started, find them everywhere. *'Look, Mummy, it's a big "O",'* said one little boy when he saw his new, circular paddling pool. Parents can help here, making the learning fun. A telegraph pole looks like a 'T', a snake curls around like an 'S'. Children love to write large letters on wet sand on the beach. Their own natural curiosity, combined with their healthy instinct to experiment, probably provides the best key of all to good experiences with letters.

What about figures?

The same principle applies to figures. Young children can learn their 'own' number (age) and for fun, find it on the calendar and other places, and look forward to 'changing from three to four' when their birthday comes. None of this instruction needs to take place in a 'teacher-pupil' way. In fact, this would probably spoil it. This sort of learning should happen incidentally, while everyday family life is going on.

Symbols – letters and numbers – are everywhere. Think of supermarkets, buses, street signs! The opportunity for a little 'fringe' learning is almost *always* present.

Security and confidence

When young children move into the unfamiliar world of school, new behaviour is expected of them. They need to be sure of themselves as people who matter if they are to be able to handle the challenges they will meet. When the going gets tough and self-doubt creeps in, they need their families to give them love and good humour, to relieve their tension. They need to feel that their family has confidence in them if they are to try again. They need to believe that success is not beyond them.

Most children learn to read even though teachers use very different methods. But very few children learn to read without some struggle. Now and then the task seems hard. Then it is the confident children who keep trying, because they know they have won through in the past. If children have been made to feel like failures, they will expect to fail when something looks strange and new. The children who have been encouraged with patience and praise will take those experiences to school, which will give them a feeling of confidence time and time again in the tasks that lie ahead.

Doesn't children's health sometimes hold them back at school, and earlier?

Yes, it certainly can and parents are the best people to watch for signs that something is wrong – not with obvious anxiety, which might make the children anxious also, but with quiet observation. Is their eyesight good? Do they hear normally with both ears? Ear trouble interferes with language learning. Even in families where the standard of childcare is high, parents may be astonished to discover only when a child is having difficulty with reading that there is a problem with one or other of these senses.

Poor diet is not always associated with low income; often parents need to look closely at family eating habits if their children are not to suffer. Poor eating often leads to fatigue and the lowering of resistance to infection; and lowered intelligence can accompany malnutrition. Recent research has found considerable evidence that regular breakfast consumption improved academic performance.

In families where all these factors are considered, some children will, nonetheless, be more frail and have more frequent illnesses than others. These children need special thought, as well as special attention and treatment. If children are physically weaker or physically disabled, help them to compensate by developing habits and hobbies which may allow them to forge ahead intellectually, to understand the world even if they cannot move around it easily. All too often 'missing school' is given later as an excuse for poor reading and low achievement. Make the extra time spent at home an opportunity for *more* conversation, *more* stories read aloud, *more* games played. Make sure that other family members understand the child's need for involvement with people and for one-to-one help in mastering skills. Astonishing results have been achieved by families who would not accept the gloomy predictions of professionals.

What about children who are disabled intellectually?

Intellectual disabilities are harder than any other sort of disability to assess in babyhood, and perhaps hardest of all for parents to accept. These children's needs are exactly those of all children, but they may be harder to meet. The children themselves need love, acceptance, humour and the opportunity to learn. Your satisfaction in the children will be in proportion to your investment in their care. An 18-month-old who had just learned to clap her hands after weeks of teaching delighted her parents. Their 'normal' baby learned this skill, almost unnoticed, and certainly untaught, at eight months. But *real* joy was attached to this achievement by the 18-month-old child who had needed much more support to be successful.

Don't assume that the child will never read. Make books a part of life from earliest babyhood. Books can be one of your tools in forging a relationship with the child. Whatever level the child can possibly reach will be more accessible to him or her with your care. Let books be a joyful help to you both.

The need for challenges

We all want our children to succeed, to be prepared for the challenges that face everyone in life. Failing in this early stage can start to set a pattern.

Children need the experience of success; it is important to arrange challenges that they can meet. A 10- or 12-piece jigsaw puzzle may be beyond a child at the stage he or she is at; a much simpler one will give the child a feeling of success, and keep the child *liking* jigsaw puzzles. Harder ones will be conquered in the future – but not if children have decided that, on jigsaw puzzles, they are failures.

If the early experience has been rewarding, children will try and try again. If, on the other hand, they have been 'allowed' to fail continually on small undertakings, and particularly if they sense your anxiety or disappointment over their level of achievement, they may well refuse to try for fear of failing again.

All too often, such children later feel threatened by the possibility of failing with reading. Sensing adult opinion that reading is *very* important, they may pretend boredom, deride the task as too young for them, recast themselves as 'physical' types who want only to climb trees or throw balls. In short, they adopt a face-saving line of action which separates them from books.

What should a parent do in this case?

Parents need sensitivity here. A child who is anxious about reading is a child at risk, and needs a crash course in acceptance and love. Comparison of different children's attainments, too many anxious enquiries about a particular child's progress, ill-judged home teaching (often using up precious time which could otherwise be devoted to story reading or interesting conversation) can all slow down, rather than speed up, progress.

This is not to underestimate the help that supportive parents can give a child who is found to be having real difficulties. Parents who are in tune with their child's way of learning, who are prepared to be patient and interested without being anxious or judging, can be the very people to give the individual time and attention that a child needs.

You may feel that you have not given your child enough attention in the past. Better late than never is a safe policy! Remember, young children *want* to be like their parents. If you read, your young son or daughter will want to copy you, but they need to be 'plugged in and switched on' early in life if the habit is to endure. Tragically, people who learn to read later in life seldom become mature readers, with all the satisfaction this term implies. True, their lives may be transformed by the ability to read simple prose, instructions, directories, street names and the like – it must never be thought to be too late to learn to read – but think what pleasures such a person has missed. We want more than this for our up-and-coming generation of children.

Books, books, books
three

There is clear evidence that it matters more what children themselves bring to the task of learning to read than what the teacher has to offer them. In fact, if a child comes to the task not sufficiently equipped, the teacher is obliged to try to make up for this lack of resources before real reading instruction can begin; and how hard this is.

It amounts to this, which I hope parents will commit to memory and make an important operating principle: *In reading, what the brain says to the eye matters more than what the eye says to the brain.* The principle is that a child needs a mind that is well-stocked, a mind that is active; and it means that parents have a responsibility to help their children develop this sort of mind.

This is where children's storybooks come in. There is no substitute for reading and telling stories to children, from the very earliest days.

Cushla and Carol

It seems that a child is never too young to be introduced to books. Cushla, a multiply disabled, chronically ill baby who needed constant care, was shown pictures in books and read to from four months of age. Her progress through a babyhood and early childhood overshadowed with illness, and dotted with crises, confounded doctors who had predicted a future of severe retardation for her.

Today, years later, Cushla has all her original handicaps, as well as several more recently discovered ones. She wears two hearing aids and thick glasses. The doctors were certainly not wrong about her disabilities. Their predictions fell down because they had no way of knowing that Cushla's family would make sure that her contact with language and books became a central part of her life. No one had to 'teach' Cushla the mechanics of reading. In a climate of language and stories, Cushla *learned* – and has profited ever since from her accomplishment.

A healthy child's interaction with books is recorded in a fascinating diary kept by a mother from the time her daughter was two years old until school entry at five. *Books Before Five* by Dorothy Neal White is an important book which is, regrettably, out of print. It might seem dated to many modern readers, but children don't change, and the message is there. Through its pages, one follows Carol's almost daily contact with new ideas, fresh situations, and previously unknown words and concepts. When Carol was just over two, her mother wrote:

> The experience makes the book richer, and the book enriches the personal experience even at this level. I am astonished at the early age this backward and forward flow between books and life takes place. With adults or older children, one cannot observe it so easily, but here at this age when all a child's experiences are known and the books read are shared, when the voluble gabble which in her speech reveals all the associations, the interaction is seen very clearly.

How to get books

First books are, of course, picture books, but parents of very young children are usually at a stage when the available money will hardly stretch to all the necessities, let alone luxuries. Perhaps you are on the way to seeing books as high on the list, but this may take time. Let's face the obvious question: How can parents afford to provide their children with enough books at the earliest level?

Libraries cater more and more for the needs of the very young child. (This, in itself, is proof that it is now recognised that books matter to children.) However, many parents are reluctant to borrow from libraries because they fear that their toddlers may damage books. This is such a near-certainty that librarians just have to accept it, and do, increasingly. Parental care can usually help, but the honest wear and tear occasioned by clumsy, over-eager little hands is expected and accepted cheerfully in the best children's departments of public libraries.

The attitude of the public has changed too. One day recently, I was choosing my own books in our fine new suburban library. It was school holiday time, and from the children's department – large, airy and very well stocked – came the cheerful noise of children's voices, laughter, and the odd clatter and bang. Libraries, of course, now have blocks, puzzles, toys and child-sized furniture. No one – librarians, borrowers, browsers, or elderly patrons sitting with magazines in comfortable chairs – seemed even to notice. Several small children seen trotting up to the desk with their books under their arms received indulgent smiles, in fact, as they passed.

Some libraries sell their own labelled book bags quite cheaply, or you can make one for your child. This helps the youngest feel that they are in charge of their very own library books. They soon learn to distinguish their borrowed books from their own, with encouragement.

MEG
Pip

Starting the library habit early is one of the very best things you can do to establish the reading habit in your children's lives. Your own willingness to share library visits and read their books aloud to them in the early days – or later days, if this habit lasts – will bring riches into both your lives.

> Simon and his 10-year-old son were recently seen both sprawled on a sofa, reading different *Tintin* books. From time to time each drew the other's attention to something hilarious or ridiculous that just had to be shared, in his book, and the laughter was contagious: truly the way to maintain a father-son relationship.

Homemade books – and stories

The littlest children will thoroughly enjoy a homemade book. A scrapbook with colourful pictures cut from magazines and other sources and stuck in place, with easy captions underneath, will seem a very personal book. You may be surprised at the interest this has for the child. It will be shown to visitors proudly, as this child's very own possession – unique too.

Don't forget about 'made up' stories, told spontaneously as the need arises. Often, these stories become family favourites, requested again and again. Naturally, the characters include the child who is listening, wide-eyed and delighted when 'who should come round the corner with his friend the dragon but Harry!'

> **A HINT:**
> Two guaranteed subjects for entertaining three- and four-year-olds in my family were: something we as *parents* had done when we were very small or something the child in question had done. The youngest child loved the account of the time she was at the family table in her highchair when they were all eating fruit and custard. It was suddenly noticed that she was wearing her bowl (fortunately nearly empty) as a hat! And a little son who once walked over the edge of the porch and rolled down the hill enveloped in a very large cardboard carton rejoiced in this story. You are sure to have some of your own available.

The conversation which arises from this one-to-one story session is a priceless asset. Any way of increasing child-adult language contact should be valued. It is here that a child learns the way in which language *works*, the ways in which ideas may be considered, modified, expanded ... You will soon find them telling *you* stories!

Always encourage your children to express their ideas, and try to listen respectfully, however falteringly they speak. You can help with interested questions which will depend on what you know of them and their individual capacity. *'That must have been exciting! What happened next?'* may be all that is necessary to keep a rather bumbling recount of an incident at kindergarten going. The keynote is 'interest', against a background of *time* and *attention*, allowing them to experiment with ways of saying what they want to communicate.

Paperbacks will help

The modern paperback publishing industry has transformed book-ownership for millions of people throughout the world, not the least of them children. A very large range of excellent, beautifully illustrated books is now available and these are, in contrast to hard-covered picture books, on sale in many local stores and shops.

The very reasonable price of these books brings them within the range of all families who are determined to provide books for their children. Careful covering (with clear adhesive plastic, to preserve the cover illustration and title) and judicious reinforcing and repair with clear sticky tape inside can prolong the life and attractiveness of picture paperbacks and ensure that the initial cost is justified.

Hard-covered books

But owning a beautiful hard-covered book is important too. A good collection of nursery rhymes, an anthology of simple stories, an alphabet book and a counting book; these are bread-and-butter items which young children should have on hand always. New books, some of which they may have met for the first time through the library, will be worth the use of family funds, from time to time.

Two children in one family loved *Mike Mulligan and His Steam Shovel* when they were

about four and three. They met the book first from the library. They renewed it and renewed it. In vain did the mother explain that other children might like to borrow it. In the end, she managed to buy a copy, not an easy feat in Auckland back then. She was almost tempted to give the *new* copy to the library, as they had really left their mark on the old!

The children are grown up now but a battered copy of *Mike Mulligan* still graces the family shelves and is enjoyed by a new generation; and several phrases from that well-loved story still occur in the family's private language.

A beloved, well-produced book will be treasured and kept. Strangely enough, for all their apparent frailty, children's hardback books do tend to survive. In many homes they are there still, years after the dolls' buggies, toys, bikes and scooters of childhood have disappeared. Battered perhaps, scruffy after years of loving and none-too-careful handling, but still there.

Listening to stories

You may agree that books are 'good for young children', but wonder about how this works towards reading. For example, how exactly does listening to stories help children when they later start to learn to read?

It is certain that listening to stories expands the vocabulary. The speech of children who are used to 'book language' is often rich and varied. This is easy to understand; such children have a large stock of words and ideas to draw on. This stock just has to help when they are later trying to make sense of a line of print. They need resources to call on, then. How can a beginning reader, groping for a word, find it unless it is in his or her mind to begin with?

> Jessica had been at school for a week and was glorying in her apparent ability to 'read'. Lying on the floor at home, with admiring family around her, she flipped over the pages of her early reader.
>
> *'This is a red ball,'* she said with confidence.
>
> *'This is a red door.'*
>
> *'This is a red coat.'*
>
> The next page showed a red van, and this stopped her in her tracks. It wasn't a *car* and it wasn't a *truck* ... Her gaze swung backwards and forwards between the picture and the text. It settled on the text and she was seen to be conjuring up all her resources. An older sister was called Vicky, so she knew.
>
> *'V ... This is a red "vehicle"!'* she triumphantly shouted.

Wrong? Let's just report that this was a child who learned to read very quickly, a child whose mind *was* well-equipped with words and ideas. Remember, *what the brain says to the eye is very important.*

There is another major way in which the child who is used to hearing stories read aloud is helped towards reading. Has it ever occurred to you that 'book language' is quite different from the spoken language of everyday conversation? Not the actual words, but their arrangement in sentences and paragraphs. When we are chatting to one another, we constantly break off, gesture with our hands, alter or enlarge our meaning by the use of facial expressions, change the direction our sentence is taking, all without losing our listener's understanding. This is because the person we are talking to is picking up cues from our total behaviour, not merely our speech.

Books, on the other hand, have to rely upon words and sentences alone, and so the language is arranged in a particular way – a way with which the child needs to be familiar. Children are used to it if they have been read to, constantly, since babyhood. In fact, this accounts for the fact that many 'well-read-to' young children speak in more complex sentences than children who have had to rely on spoken language alone for their example.

Another tool: poetry

All children love rhymes, jingles, songs and simple poems. They have an amazing capacity for learning them by heart, and this helps them to cope with words they might not meet anywhere else. It can also help them to learn to read, if they are used to looking at the verse on the page.

An interesting story was told by a friend in England some years ago. Her first child was on the verge of reading when she started school, and seemed from that point to 'teach herself'. Her younger brother, from the same bookish background, seemed to make no progress at school, and the teacher informed his parents of this.

> Mark's mother (a secondary school teacher of Latin and Greek who had never thought about 'teaching reading') decided she should try to help him. On impulse she seized the family collection of nursery rhymes and said to Mark, *'Let's read this together.'* Of course, he knew the rhymes by heart, but his mother underlined the words as they both read them. Then Mark did it by himself, matching what was in his head to the words on the page. In a very short time, he could launch himself onto other texts, and did so.
>
> *'There you are,'* said his mother. *'You can read.'*
>
> *'I didn't know that was reading,'* said Mark.

Very significant words! This little boy had not grasped that reading was 'getting the message'. He was struggling with a word-by-word system, with dismal results. His older sister had already decided what had to be done, and had done it, as many a bright child has.

This is a true story. Later Mark was accepted into Oxford University and ultimately became a noted scholar; but at the age of six, he was failing in a system which was actually preventing him from 'learning to read'.

There are many good collections of poetry for the young. Even before children can say the poems, they love supplying the last word. Together you might try to build up a repertoire to use in the car, and other places of possible boredom. Some picture books, too, have a rhyming text, and many of these are *very* memorable: *'… Hairy Maclary from Donaldson's Dairy …'*

When reading begins at school, imagine a child who has never heard fairy stories read aloud trying to decipher *'Once upon a time'*! Having patterns of book language in the mind to fit language into is just as important as knowing what the words mean.

Any teacher of 'new entrants' will tell you that there is a huge difference between the children who have listened to stories read aloud since babyhood and those who have had no book experience at all. Some will be used to handling books, know where they start and end, and be familiar with the sight of print.

At the other extreme, some children will seldom, if ever, have handled a book at all. It makes sense to have your children included in the first group, as this is the one that leaps ahead; not because the children are really different, but because someone has given them the opportunity to absorb facts about books, print and language. Children in the second group, through no fault of their own, have been penalised.

The connection may not be immediately clear, but it is there nonetheless. It is only too well recognised by teachers and social workers.

Books without pictures

Beautifully illustrated books are a priceless part of children's lives and will be enjoyed for much of their early school life but I believe that giving young children the experience of listening to a story from a book which is *not* illustrated is good practice for later reading. After all, one is not truly reading until the eyes skim along the line while meaning pours into the mind. Giving children practice on *one* part of this process, before they can read themselves, is a very useful exercise.

To steal a phrase from a child who said she was 'making the pictures in my head', we suggest that *you* suggest this to your listening child. To make it a real game, you can even ask your child to close his or her eyes, and later tell you how it worked. A three-year-old with eyes tightly clenched said excitedly, *'I'm doing it, Daddy – it works!'*

These days, our lives are so crammed with visual images that we need to see this over-abundance as a threat to our children's imaginations. To read smoothly, and with enjoyment, we *must* 'make pictures in our heads'. This is the essence of 'responsive reading' – the kind we want for all our children.

Will all these things really help children to learn to read?

We sincerely believe that they will, and we base this belief on many years of caring for, teaching, living with and observing children. There are, of course, other factors that help children towards learning to read, and others which may make the task difficult. Some of these have already been noted, but the richness a child finds in listening to stories read aloud by a loving adult will smooth any path, lighten any load.

Take heart

Where goodwill is combined with sensible, constructive practice, wonders can be achieved. Children with very real handicaps, both physical and intellectual, can realise their full potential, whatever this may be, and be happy and self-accepting, in a loving, encouraging setting. Some of them will surprise everyone with their attainments.

Well-equipped children will flourish, given the same favourable environment, but also have pressing needs. More will be required of them; and whatever path they follow, the ability to read fluently and responsively is the first and foremost demand society will make.

We believe that the suggestions made in this book will help parents to set their young children on the path to reading. If parents have also been helped to understand something of the real nature of reading, this will be a considerable advantage when their children start school. If they have also been persuaded that reading means books and have adopted the read-aloud habit and the library habit, wonders may well be achieved; and not merely in the world of school.

Other experiences, especially play

Children need opportunities to arrange their own lives, to organise their own experiences, and establish order in their own world; and this implies the freedom to do this. What has this to do with reading? In the end, no one can help the reader. Children must explore the text, respond to it, recreate the story, find their own mistakes, correct them, and read on. They must organise their own behaviour. Many of their past experiences in play will have prepared them for this control over what they are trying to do.

Play is recognised by leading authorities in the educational field as having tremendous value for children. In their play, be it with saucepans from the kitchen cupboard, sand, water, earth, blocks, cars, dolls and all the paraphernalia of housekeeping, building materials and so on, they are constantly extending their knowledge of the world and how it works. Cause and effect, comparison, trial and error, the give-and-take of relationships with other people: all are experienced and re-experienced. Children learn in play how to manipulate their environment and test their growing skills, physical, intellectual and social, against the myriad demands of their environment.

Reading as a skill requires flexibility of thought, and play experiences feed into this skill. Creativity in play translates into creativity in learning. Reading is recreating, almost without knowing one is doing it, from known words and concepts, drawing conclusions from what has gone before, looking forward with imagination to what may be expected to follow. The process is helped enormously if the child has had the opportunity to be creative in the past. Rich and varied play experiences, in the early years and later, provide this opportunity.

Modern life

Many families these days have two working parents, whereas in earlier years there would almost always have been 'a mum to come home to'. But today, even in families where the father's income would support the family, many mothers with professional qualifications feel they must keep working for the sake of their careers; or even because they believe that looking after small children would be boring, or lessen them in some way. Of course, many parents find they simply must both work, to feed their families and pay the bills. The role of the solo parent is almost always harder still.

Unfortunately there is no magic key, but read the suggestions in this book and try to put them into action as, where and when you can.

The term 'quality time' is interesting. All time is quality time to children if the interactions they are having with those who love them are happy ones. Getting them up in the morning, dressing, breakfast, riding in the car, dinner time, evening (don't even think about turning on the television), bedtime ... it is even more important for the part-time parent to manage these times in a child-centred way than it is for the full-time parent and, of course, often much harder.

Make the weekly visit to the library a treat – if *you* regard it as such, so will the children – and libraries are increasingly open in the weekends. Find out about yours, and join the family up if you haven't already. Try to make car journeys fun. Learn some simple, jingly songs and encourage everyone to sing. Surely you will know *'Old McDonald Had a Farm'* and *'The Wheels on the Bus'* to start with.

If the children are in daycare, they will probably know songs they can teach you. Make it a game – become one of those mums or dads who can get a bit of fun out of any situation: *'This old car will never get up the hill unless we all sing louder!'* Use your imagination. If the children are happy, your own life will be much easier. Remember that they need your

attention *more*, during these periods, if you must be away from them for much of the day. Don't let them feel like parcels to be picked up and carted somewhere and dumped.

And always, always ...

Sharing books will help; for relationships to develop, human beings must share ideas, and books are superlative sources of ideas. Remember: books can be bridges between children and parents, and children and the world.

I encountered the following statement some years ago. Try to remember it, in your daily dealings with your children and in all aspects of your lives together. Apart from anything else, it gives you permission to enjoy yourself with your children.

> **'To live a rich, full and satisfying life at each stage of growth is the best possible preparation for the next stage.'**

More direct instruction
four

The suggestions in this section are for parents who, for some reason or other, feel they want to take their children a little further towards reading, before they start school. They should not be used as a starting point. The foundation-building outlined in earlier chapters is essential if these ideas are to work.

Also, the steps we describe here will not conflict with instruction which the child will later encounter. There are certain things that the beginning reader has to absorb and master before progress can be made, regardless of the instruction system used. Knowing these things is certain to help, whatever system your child encounters at school.

Well, there you are with a four-year-old who has been read to, talked to and listened to since very early days. The child is speaking well, has a considerable attention span, enjoys a wide range of play experiences, and you want to take him or her a step further along the road to 'real reading'.

How do I start?

It's a good idea to observe carefully what the child *does* know about books. Adults take for granted many things that children must learn. Use this as a checklist:

- Do they know that a book starts at the front and proceeds, page by page, to the back? (Have the child show you the 'front' and the 'back'.)
- Do they know that the spoken words, as the story is read to them, arise from the black marks, the print, on the page?
- Do they know that the print must be 'read' from left to right across the page?
- Do they know that, if there is more than *one* line of print, we read the top one first, then the next down, and so on, always from the left to the right?

It helps if the child has heard terms like 'word', 'letter', 'print', and 'title' used casually during story sessions, and at other times. This happens so naturally in a 'reading' family that teaching such concepts is unnecessary. But check, nonetheless. It is surprising how easily children who are read to seem to slip into this knowledge, but there may be some confusion, which can be resolved.

You may find that the child does not want to cooperate, despite a healthy 'reading' background. No matter. Many children with a fund of this sort of knowledge, children who have not received any 'instruction' before school, leap away to a fine start when school begins.

> On Emma's first day at school, the children were asked to draw a picture showing something they had done in the holidays. The teacher then wrote a sentence, dictated by the children, under each picture. On arrival home Emma proudly showed her mother a picture under which the teacher had written 'I went on an escalator in a big shop.' *'That word says "escalator",'* Emma told her mother confidently, pointing correctly.
>
> *'How do you know?'* asked her mother. *'Because "escalator" is a big word, and that word is the biggest,'* said Emma.

This five-year-old had had no preschool instruction in reading, but had been read to constantly. Obviously, 'a word' was a recognisable unit of print on the page to Emma. It was possible to make inferences from existing knowledge, and she did so.

Back to the four-year-old whom we introduced at the beginning of this section. You have checked his or her understanding of the 'book facts' we have just listed, found them in satisfactory shape, and decide to proceed. We suggest the following steps for the parent:

- Choose a familiar book with a brief and very easy text, clearly displayed on the page. As an alternative, or as well, you might like to make your own book, perhaps using the child's ideas for the text. But *keep it very, very simple*; preferably one short sentence occupying one line on each page, with related pictures. (Many parents choose material that is far too difficult.)
- Read several pages slowly to the child, running your finger smoothly under the words, to match your voice.
- Increase the number of pages treated in this way as you judge the child's interest to be increasing.
- Read several different and very easy books (printed or homemade) in this way, repeating the performance and reusing the same books as often as the child seems interested.

If all is going well you should now be able to progress to the following:

- Using one of the now-familiar books, choose a short sentence and have the child repeat this after you, while you underline the words with your finger. (If possible, for this first attempt, find a page with one simple sentence only on it.) Initially, do this for only one or two pages. Gradually increase the number of pages for which the child joins in, but only if his or her interest in helping increases.

- Read several books in this way, and reread the old ones.
- The next step may be taken spontaneously by the child, or you may suggest it; that is, that the child might use a finger to underline the words while saying them, after you.

Remember, however, that the young child may not have sufficient control of small muscles to do this, or may tire easily. No matter. Knowing that this has something to do with stories and reading is enough.

If you feel yourself getting discouraged, angry or impatient, negative in any way, do give up and return to story sessions only. Remember that reading is an extremely complicated act, and that you probably think it a great deal simpler for your child than it is. At all costs you must avoid associating learning to read with unpleasantness, strain or boredom.

Finish with a read-aloud story

It is a sound idea to finish each 'teaching' session with a *real* story (*not* a graded reader) of the child's choice. If you are handling things well, the child might delight everyone by ultimately finding a familiar word or expression quite spontaneously in one of the picture books. This is fine if it happens but pressing for it may spoil the relaxed pleasure the child has always had from stories, and do more harm than good.

This stage can be maintained for a considerable period of time. In fact the benefits will increase with repetition. The child will be constantly *drawing his or her own conclusions* about letters, words and sentences, and the way they all fit together to tell stories.

The following anecdote was supplied by a parent who suddenly realised that her child had been doing exactly this. She had certainly had no intention of 'teaching' him.

> Daniel loved *Davy's Day* from babyhood, and would often ask for it even after he had turned three – particularly when he was tired. Each page has a simple statement about Davy's everyday doings, near the top of the page. (The text is consistently on the left page, with picture on the right.) On most pages there is one word at the bottom of the page, well away from the rest of the text, which gives a lead into the sentence on the next page. On four of the pages this word is 'and', on another four 'or', and on two pages 'then'. On one single page, right at the end of the book, the two words 'and soon' occur in this position. I had always stressed them for expression really. To my astonishment, when he was about three I discovered one day that Daniel knew these words. Several times, he found them in other books we were reading together.
>
> I thought of trying to teach him more words, but couldn't be bothered! He seemed to be learning words and expressions constantly from our read-aloud sessions – I think I have always been inclined to point to the print as I read.
>
> I love books myself and have always read a lot to the children. It's so much more peaceful than what goes on if I let them get bored and bad-tempered!

In case you think I am relating only success stories, let me tell you about an experience with a grandchild many years ago.

> Nicola was four, and I could tell from reading to her and listening to her that she was well on the way to reading herself. I found a short 'reader' which stressed the word 'little' and read it to her. The first time was a success; she liked the story about the *'little old man and the little old woman and their collection of little old animals'*, and did not suspect my intentions.
>
> Next time through, I underlined the text with my finger and then pointed out 'little'. Nicky was still, at least, polite and didn't complain. Next day I produced the book again and asked casually, *'Can you see that word "little"?'* Nicky did not bother to be polite this time. *'Yes, I can see it all over the place and I don't like it!' I want you to read me* The House of Four Seasons*!'* (This was her favourite at the time.) The book is long out of print but I still have that copy, and it reminds me of Nicola every time I see it.
>
> As we settled down with the requested title she said, as if to clinch the deal, *'Anyway, I don't like those floppy books. I only like real books!'* I gave up; and the next year her teacher apparently had no similar difficulties. Nicky was reading fluently in no time.

Just to vary the theme:

> A teacher in Australia told me about her small grandson who always stared fixedly at the illustrations as she read a picture book to him. Wanting to draw his attention to the print, she asked him, *'What do you think this is for, Michael?' 'Oh,'* said Michael airily, *'that's just for people who can't read the pictures!'*

So be prepared; children will surprise you. (The little boy above was clearly in need of enlightenment, which his grandmother provided, she reported!)

Also, you may be faced by a question you can't answer.

> I was about to start reading a new picture book to a four-year-old grandson. The book had very attractive endpapers. I pointed them out to Oliver, turning to the back of the book to show him that they were repeated there.
>
> He was obviously interested, and turned back and forward several times, looking closely at the design (small animals in neat rows, each line moving on, so that the animals all went diagonally down the page). I thought it was the animals that were absorbing Oliver's interest, but he suddenly said, *'Why aren't the ones at the beginning called start papers?'*

Where do I go from here?

Some parents may still feel they want to involve their children in a more definite teaching programme, and might like to introduce 'the sentence game' at this stage. Here's how to go about it.

- Make a very small number of 'word cards', using ordinary cardboard. The back of a used writing pad will do well; cut long strips about 25 mm deep and snip off the length you need for each word.
- Use simple words which will have meaning and interest for your child. For example, if you have a boy and a girl, you might try these words: Ben / Grace / is / a / boy / girl.
- Next, arrange the cards to make a sentence, encouraging the child to help. The first sentence should feature the child's own name: *'Ben is a boy.'*

The second will, of course, be *'Grace is a girl.'* Without any more cards, you can have some fun. Let the child correct you when you write *'Ben is a girl'* or *'Grace is a boy.'* In a very short time, the child will differentiate between 'boy' and 'girl' and be able to select the other words as needed.

The children may like to keep the words in a box or tin, using them whenever they wish. When you use the words, use them only in sentences, to preserve the 'message' value of print.

Now continue, using your own family situation and consolidating *always* before adding more words. If your family (or a relative's or neighbour's family) includes a baby – or a cat, dog or other pet – you have plenty of opportunity to extend the game without changing its form:

'Jack is a baby.'
'Spot is a dog.'

This might be a good time to point out that they really need more 'is' and 'a' cards – a painless way of helping them to realise that these small words occur very often in English.

The word 'and', of course, is the obvious next choice, so that they can join two or more sentences together.

Once they are really used to making these sentences, another 'form' can be introduced. Once again, it can be fun:

'Ben likes cake.'
'Jack likes milk.'
'Spot likes bones.'

The words in these new sentences can then be interchanged, while the word 'likes' and the names of various foods are learned.

Inevitably, the child will ask you to make more cards – and some of them will not be very simple words at all! Some children want to start making their own cards quite soon. A four-year-old we know was so insistent upon this that her mother started cutting up cereal packets into very large cards so that her daughter could print on them with her crayons. Later, this child even cut her own cards. Their uneven shapes, with her very wobbly printing, proved no hindrance to learning. In the end, they were all housed in a large cardboard carton.

You will have the idea by now, and will be able to introduce new forms gradually. You might try 'is' (card already familiar) followed by an adjective: *'Ben is big', 'Jack is little', 'Spot is black.'*

You can see that the next words might be 'not' and 'very'. But, stay with simple and easy texts; don't let it become complicated. Enterprising children can play the game together, or with an adult. Before long, quite lengthy sentences emerge.

We would expect four-year-olds to forget as easily as they learn and not always to know tomorrow what they knew yesterday. This should not worry you or the child.

Do not expect that this skill in sentence making and word selecting, or an interest in letters, will immediately carry over into reading books. Children differ greatly here, and many who seem slow to make the transfer become excellent readers in the end. The value of this contact with the way written language works to convey meaning to the reader will not be lost; it is fundamental to the reading process.

The rule is to introduce words *in sentences* always, encouraging the child to use a full range of cues and clues to get the meaning from print. This is what reading is all about.

A note of caution: Don't institute the sentence game *instead* of the 'reading together' sessions described earlier in this chapter. Continue with both, simultaneously, if they are being enjoyed.

More importantly, don't use up precious time on either, at the expense of reading aloud from exciting picture books. Knowing beyond any doubt that reading is fun is the only certain inducement for the child to keep going.

Parents' questions
five

In this chapter we will try to answer some of the questions parents ask about modern teaching methods, and about their own role in their children's education. Many of the answers (and questions) involve repetition of what has gone before, but we feel this does not matter; if a point is worth making it is worth making *twice* (at least).

Parents are, understandably, puzzled about methods they do not understand. Often they feel that there is no method being used. Many parents have these doubts. Because they sat in desks at an earlier period and worked steadily through a reading scheme, they feel this is the right way. *'We learned this way,'* they say. *'What's wrong with it?'*

The answers in this section are based on the proposition that teaching methods should fit in with, and support, the learning process at every stage. We hope that no one will have any quarrel with that.

Is the teaching of reading today quite different from what it was 50 years ago?

Not really. Dramatic claims are often made, and people may be persuaded to believe that children were once 'really taught' to read, in a serious way, whereas now teachers 'play around' with 'new methods'.

In the days when 'phonics' as a method was said to be used exclusively, this was not so. Anyone who is 70 and over will be able to remember labelled pictures on the wall, the new word each day used in a sentence, illustrated books with stories in them, and many other 'aids'. In the same way, during the *'Janet and John'* or *'Dick and Jane'* era of the 1950s when whole words were emphasised, teachers found they naturally drew children's attention to letters and sounds. The children would otherwise have had a serious handicap in attacking new words.

What we do hope is that teachers today are using sensibly the findings of modern research on reading. The best features of all the so-called 'methods' have value and a place in a well-balanced programme. Labels like 'phonic' methods or 'look-and-say' methods are too simple. They distort the rich programmes they are supposed to describe.

How do children learn to identify new words?

Only a few new words are introduced at a time, and the teacher arranges a series of learning steps. To begin with, the teacher will make sure the children know what each word means. Then the teacher will read a story containing the new words, so that the children hear them in the context of a message. That is their 'real' place.

When the children then read the same material, they are prepared for the new words, and are able to succeed in recognising them. When reading aloud material that contains a new word they have not been prepared for, the children will be encouraged to anticipate what the new word might be. The structure of the sentence and the sense of the story often lead to a correct idea. If the children check on the first letter of the word as well, they will usually be correct in their response. We do this all the time as adult readers. You can

catch yourself at it, next time you are reading a newspaper article in which a few words, or a whole line of print, have been omitted. But the teacher is not merely letting the children guess when he or she invites them to try a word they have not met before. The teacher will not be content even if they are correct. The teacher is then likely to say, *'Are you right? How did you know?'* encouraging the children to look closely at the method they used to identify the word. Perhaps they knew the first letter, and guessed; perhaps they also sensed that the word's 'sounded' length matched its written length. They may have done these things without knowing they did. This happens all the time in a complex mental operation like reading. Identifying the method they used may help them to use it again, extending and modifying their method as they go.

More details

If you have not thought about this process before, you might like to have a little more detail about how it works. We might call it the 'new-word identification process'.

The first clues that a child picks up about a new word come from the sentence itself. *'The boy hit the ...' 'The old man climbed ... up the hill.'* The missing word in the first sentence will be a noun. In the second sentence the word will probably be an adverb ending in 'ly'. Of course, children at this stage do not understand the words 'noun' and 'adverb', but they use them in their speech constantly, in the correct places. A two-year-old might say *'I kick ball hard'*, with verb, noun and adverb all in the right places. He or she is still learning to speak but is well on the way to knowing the correct order of words in English. This is a huge advantage when children are learning to read.

Even without the story to help us we might guess that the first sentence needs a word like 'ball', or 'stone', or something like 'boy', or 'thief', or as a long shot, 'teacher'! It can only be one of a very few words. In the second sentence the most likely word is probably 'slowly', but you could think of others.

When one is reading a story, a new word can only be one of a small number of words. (We forget this when we think that reading is being able to read words in isolation.)

Back to the child

Now, if the child reader notices that the first sentence was *'The boy hit the b...'*, he or she is using a 'first letter' clue. There may only be two or three likely words to fit everything the child has noticed so far. At the same time the child considers word length, without actually counting letters and discards 'bed' and 'balloon'. The child's eye picks up the last letter 'l' and putting it all together he or she says 'bell'. This might be wrong, because the boy may have been playing with a tennis racquet, and our reader would then have a sentence that did not make sense with other parts of the story. If so the child would probably take a closer look, say the word slowly letter by letter (or letter group by letter group) and discover for himself or herself the point of the error.

This sounds complicated but it isn't. You may have noticed that it works a little like the game 'Twenty Questions', because each bit of information reduces the number of ideas to be considered; and the brain works very fast in sorting out the possibilities.

What could our reader have learned?

This may well have been a critical experience for the child. It may have taught the child that first and last letters are not entirely reliable, and that it is important to work slowly from left to right across a word to distinguish it from a very similar word ('bell', 'ball').

What might you have learned from this example? That there are many, many occasions when one is reading text when it is not necessary to take in all the information. Like the 'Twenty Questions' game, one does not always need all the questions.

You may think 'What a complicated way to teach. Why not just teach children to sound the letters, or recognise the words?' *There is a vast amount of evidence to convince us that the brain works on reading in this way and that it does this whatever teaching programme is used.* It matters not what method the teachers adopt; observers find children act in this way regardless.

This is the way adults read. It is a way by which very young children who don't know many words can read interesting but simple stories. Children can add to their own knowledge if they approach print in this way, and that is very important. Children still have to know a great deal about letter-sound relationships, and they go on learning this for some years. They learn eventually to recognise words in a flash, but that is because they have read them so many times. The words are very familiar to them.

How do children ever learn to read without learning their letters, or sounds, first?

Most reading specialists believe that it is important for the reader to think about 'the message' from the beginning. Before they make any real progress, children have to know that reading *means* 'getting the message'. This is why teachers arrange for them to experience the process at a very early stage through using the simple little 'early reading' books we have described. As soon as the children have this feeling for the task in hand, the teacher will start directing their attention to letters, sounds, and parts of words. Before long, 'real reading books' will extend their experience of the way these units work together to produce messages which can be understood.

Over the next few years, most children will build up a vast experience of letter-sound relationships, and the patterns of language written down.

Learning to read is planned to be an interesting and satisfying experience. The idea is to have material full of meaning from the start so that children are stimulated to think about what they are reading. This is not pandering to children. It is not sugar-coating the pill. It is merely making sensible use of what is known about the process of learning to read.

Also, in the writing they are doing, children are working with letters and the true sounds of language all the time. If you like to put it that way, *they are using phonics from the very beginning. They are finding ways to represent the sounds they can hear, in print.*

What if my child seems slow to move on from this early stage?

Parents do not worry too much if their children are a little slow to walk or cut their teeth. They accept this as part of the range of individual differences among children. For the same kinds of reasons some children will be slower to reach the stage where they can begin to learn to read. Children differ quite markedly in the speed and ease with which they learn to read.

It helps the child who is moving slowly if parents can feel comfortable about individual differences and neither worry about it themselves nor worry the child about it. Don't make an issue of it. Encourage the child, give praise for what he or she can do, protect him or her from the jibes of brothers and sisters and unhappy comparisons. Talk the situation over with the teacher and help the child to make real progress, little by little, however gradual. Don't panic, push or show anxiety. Forcing the pace will not help and may do great damage. The child can only proceed from where he or she is. And most importantly, keep reading interesting books to your children. You will not only be increasing their vocabulary and their knowledge of the patterns of English; you will be showing them that reading as an occupation is well worth aiming for!

Should I hear the child's reading at home?

Opinions differ about the usefulness of hearing reading at home and you should be guided by the school's views. If you are expected to help, you should consult the teacher about what you and your child can do together. At all costs, resolve to make it relaxed, even 'fun', not a 'duty' session. Be positive and helpful when the child is 'stuck':

Pause, and let the child solve the problem.
Say *'Would you like me to help?'*
Prompt with *'What would make sense?'*
Or *'Let's go back here and try again'.*
Or *'Would you like me to tell you?'*
Or *'Have you looked at this part?'*

Praise the child if he or she solves the problem, or comes close, or just has a go. If the going gets too difficult, offer to read a few pages. The child will read it better tomorrow if he or she has heard how it all goes together today. It is easy to sound as if you are trying to catch them out instead of helping them!

Use your own judgement about whether you should abandon the session, particularly if you feel that, despite your best intentions, a note of strain is creeping into the encounter.

Finally, always read aloud from an enjoyable picture book or collection of stories at the end of the session.

If hearing the child's reading doesn't go well, or I don't like the idea, is there an alternative?

Yes there is. You could try the 'Reading with' way, the method recommended to parents of the Reading Centre children. Many of these parents were already tense about what they felt was their children's reading failure, and I did not want to risk a 'question and answer' session between parent and child. Here's how it goes.

Child and parent sit comfortably, close together, holding the book so that each can see it easily. Parent says *'Let's read it together'*, or something similar, and starts to read, moving his or her finger smoothly along under the text. To begin with the child's voice is probably just behind the adult's, but often the child is able to take over, and get slightly ahead. The trick is to recognise where children *can* manage and let them take over. But if there is doubt, do it for them or pause and let them try if they clearly want to.

This procedure may sound like the 'helping' method described earlier, but is different in an important way. In the 'Reading with' method, the child is not questioned in any way, and is not allowed to fail. The adult's voice is always there; the pause to allow the child to say a word or a group of words, if he or she obviously wants to, is almost unnoticeable. You'll get the knack of this quite quickly, and it is a very friendly procedure which will not be over-challenging to the child – or over-taxing to you.

What should I do if, despite everything, I feel very concerned that my child is not making progress in the first year?

If you are really concerned, the teacher may let you observe him or her teaching your child at school. You may well be able to help at home, but if your child finds reading difficult then it is very important not to confuse him or her with different methods.

Your problem is that you will have a host of personal beliefs about reading and you will set out to teach your child what you believe he or she should be learning. You certainly have the advantage of a one-to-one teaching situation, but also considerable disadvantage in being personally involved in an emotional way, which means you will get irritated rather quickly. You will find it difficult to notice when the child has solved the problem in a different or unexpected way or made a significant learning gain in an area you didn't arrange for.

The 'Reading with' method described earlier might be safer and more effective here – it gets the child into the 'swing' of reading, rather like learning to ride a bike.

Back to school

An experienced teacher will work in a flexible way to allow children who are different to approach reading along different routes. This may confuse you as a parent. Your Ryan may be doing different things from your friend's Jessica in the same classroom. Don't panic. He may be too experienced in Jessica's area to make it worth his spending time on her activities.

Shouldn't children read accurately, without any mistakes?

Well, yes, if they are already readers, but no, if they are learning to read. Errors are to be expected in the oral reading of young children and, importantly, errors can be self-instructive for the reader. This is because reading is a self-improving system that gains proficiency through practice and ongoing problem solving. The more a child reads, the better he or she becomes. This is clarified by considering what the child does after making an error.

After an error has been made, the child often recognises this and tries to correct it. This has been called self-correction. It shows you clearly that the child is applying the 'Twenty Questions' technique. It is part of the self-improving system because that is the moment when the child attends closely and discovers new things about print that he or she was overlooking before. We do it when we're reading the paper, but we do it silently.

The real goal is, of course, not accurate saying of the words but accurate reception of the message being read. The print on the page must be related by the child to some meaning from past experience. To get from print to meaning we want children, even beginning readers, to think about what they are reading, to react to it, to get ideas from it, and to link these ideas with other ideas from their memory of other experiences.

In the light of what has been said so far, should parents try to teach their preschoolers to read?

We believe that adults should proceed cautiously, using methods like those described in the last chapter. You may be surprised to hear that there are studies to show that slightly older brothers and sisters have more success teaching preschoolers to read than parents do. And this should make us ask why.

We suspect that, without giving it any thought, slightly older children assess the real nature of the task better than adults. They have more recently grappled with it themselves, perhaps. Adults, many years past this stage, are inclined to judge the wrong things to be simple. There is a message here. *We adults may be wrong about what we think the child needs to know, to read.*

Will my child start to learn to read on his or her first day at school?

From the day when the teacher first accepts your child into the class, his or her efforts will be directed towards teaching the child to read.

This is a time for settling, on your child's part, and observing on the teacher's. The teacher needs to know 'where the child is' before he or she can take the child 'somewhere else'. It is not hard to imagine the range of different levels that teachers find in new entrants. Modern teaching tries to treat each child as a person with individual needs.

Before long your child will probably work with the help of small, soft-covered books which have a picture on one page at each opening, and a few words (usually a simple phrase or sentence) on the opposite page. These books are sometimes called 'instant readers' or 'early readers' because, with the help of the picture and the first sentence of the book, the child is able to invent sentences like those in the book.

If the teacher is responding to the strengths of each child, he or she will introduce them to formal reading sessions at different times. But you can rest assured that reading as a goal for each child looms large in the teacher's mind.

What does the teacher do if the child has not had a good learning environment before school?

Your child may know a great deal about books when he or she comes to school. But not all children are well-prepared. So teachers introduce activities which allow them to observe which children can handle a book, open it, turn the pages, find and keep the place by the pictures, look from left to right across a page. The children learn how to study the details of pictures. Some have not learned to do this. They need practice at expressing in words the ideas suggested by the pictures. Their attention is directed to things that look alike and things that look different in the pictures, because they are being led towards looking for such differences in letters. Habits of noticing small differences are very important in learning words, but they are easily learned if we begin with objects and pictures rather than letters. One little line makes all the difference between 'cat' and 'eat'.

How can children learn if they are not made to sit quietly and pay attention to what the teacher says?

The atmosphere in schools is more informal today than when some of us went to school, but there is order, control and discipline which you may have a chance to observe. Many of the activities that prepare a child for reading involve talking. The teacher provides situations in which children will want to talk because they have something interesting to talk about. It is not just the willing talkers that concern the teacher. He or she must see that every child feels comfortable with language in this classroom.

As children gain experience in expressing themselves, they gain the kind of control over words that helps them to anticipate and understand the language of books. Talking things over informally before and after reading is important in helping children get the most out of what they read.

You can see that 'sitting quietly' may be the very thing that most young children do *not* need. They learn best through being involved. Modern teachers try to provide this involvement for all children.

If you do want to see a class of small children 'sitting still and paying attention', though, arrange to go along when the teacher is reading a good story aloud!

I believe that children draw pictures and try to write before they can even read at school. Is this helpful?

When children show their pictures to the teacher, the teacher will ask each child to talk about his or her picture. Then the teacher will write down the child's dictated message. The child has made the statement in pictures. He or she then puts the same message into words and the teacher writes this down. This is to help the child understand that messages can be put into print, and that print, therefore, has messages in it.

Very soon the child begins to trace the teacher's message or to copy it, and when the child is sufficiently confident he or she may begin to write some of his or her own messages. Again the teacher avoids pressure and helps whenever help is needed. The teacher praises what comes out right and overlooks much that is inaccurate. Above all, the teacher's aim is to have children who *want* to write. Why?

Writing is complementary to reading. In reading, one is trying to extract someone else's message; in writing, one is sending a message to another person. In reading, we take the meaning out of sentences, phrases and words; in writing, we build up the message from letters into words, into sentences. What children learn in writing is of great use to them in reading. So, before children can 'really read' their first book, they will probably be pestering you to help them to write letters and words. You should respond to their requests, and, like the teacher, be their scribe, or secretary. But keep it simple.

Should parents blame the school if their children have real problems with reading?

Some teachers are, of course, more capable than others, and there are difficult classes. If you feel particularly dissatisfied with the instruction that your child is receiving there are steps that you should feel able to take, like seeking a second and independent opinion, firstly within the school, from a senior teacher in the junior classes, or the principal. The school should have considerable resources to bring to your child's problem. The way you approach the school should help to gain access to these resources.

Try, always, to be friendly and positive in your approach to the school. If you still feel that your child is not making progress, there may be a teacher with special training, or a psychologist who could take an independent view of the problem. However, before blaming the school there are several things that should be thought about.

Schools receive children at least five years after birth. Scientists know, without a doubt, that these first five years are extremely important for learning and the development of intelligence. Well-prepared children seldom fail to learn to read but 'ill-equipped' children tend to go from bad to worse. Disadvantaged, they fall behind. Then, because they can't read, they become disheartened and stop trying.

All families have their 'ups and downs' and these commonly affect the children's lives and may impede progress or even bring about regression. On the other hand, a 'good year' for the family often means excellent progress for the child, sometimes despite the school.

When you change your home district you change many of the secure things in your young child's life. The child has to face a completely different set of people and school and different teacher demands. Some take it in their stride; others take time.

Schools are not able to provide teaching on a one-to-one basis. *Try* to imagine that you are a teacher with 30 children in your class, all with different needs, at different levels, with different temperaments, some with unhelpful homes and a few with physical and emotional problems. Individual help is obviously not possible for all children all the time. Most learning has to be in a group situation.

As we said earlier, well-prepared children seldom fail to learn to read and it is in the years before school that we have the opportunity to prepare our children by providing informal one-to-one learning situations in everyday life. This is where children learn their language, and learn how to learn. These experiences prepare them for further learning in a group at school.

What about television?

The short answer to this question is 'The less the better.' People who draw attention to 'good' programmes for young children are usually talking about programmes which they think are merely harmless. The fortunate youngsters have parents who talk and listen to them, read them stories, give them a full share in family life and ensure that they have access to rich play experiences. Children need to be involved, to relate closely to other people, to learn to contribute, and to respond with confidence and satisfaction. Television leads so easily to passive acceptance; questions cannot be answered by the television set and so they are not asked. Language is not like it is in conversation and so it does not encourage *listening*, images are too fragmented to foster concentration; and you cannot go back to understand what confused you the first time round.

If you really do think your children would profit from watching a particular programme, be sure to view television with them. At the end of the programme switch off the set and discuss what the child saw, encouraging an enquiring attitude.

You won't need to use the television set as a babysitter if your children have been helped to develop creative interests. Active interests are productive and constructive, just the opposite of passive viewing. Your children need to use their early years in the best possible way: for growing and learning, as a preparation for everything that lies ahead.

What about computers and things?

When computers first appeared on the public scene some years ago, there was a feeling of excitement in the air. It was rumoured that they could work magic, perform miracles. Schools would be transformed; think of what they could teach children! No one seemed to remember that 40 years before, it had been predicted that the old-fashioned one-teacher-to-one-class tradition would disappear when television invaded the schools.

Neither of these things has happened, of course. There is overwhelming evidence that children, both young and older, need a real, flesh-and-blood person to relate to, if they are going to learn. There is simply no substitute for human relationships if children are to grow to be caring, compassionate people themselves; and not least, to learn.

There need be no doubt at all that children with access to computers will acquire the skills they need in this sphere to assist with future learning. These skills are elementary, and not beyond the ability of the average child. Only a few in many thousands will become computer scientists – those brilliant people who design mysterious software. For the rest, we may relax; mastery of necessary skills is not hard. It is important to note, though, that reading skills are essential when it comes to engaging with the Internet.

What is very definite is that those children who become *real readers* perform better in any sphere (computer science included) than their companions. Those of our children who attain levels of education which will see them succeeding in their chosen careers (which will certainly involve computer use) will be those who have mastered mature reading and writing skills.

Here's a point to consider: An acquaintance in his mid-fifties teaches computer science at tertiary level. Did he have access to computers in his early life? No one did! Computers were not in general use until his early adulthood. What is true is that he has always, from early childhood, been a prolific reader.

Reading is the vital component of education, and will remain so. If you read fluently and responsively and if you make books part of your life, the world, with its choices, will be open to you.

As parents, our urgent task is to help our children reach their educational potential. At the earliest level, language shared and stories read aloud constitute the best launching pad – and keep our relationship with them healthy too!

A word of caution. There is a vast number of computer games labelled 'educational' now available for young children, and many are rubbishy. Unless you have access to sound advice it is best to avoid them. Making sure your child has plenty of opportunity to engage in the active, imaginative, *noisy*, time-honoured occupations of childhood – with plenty of stories and books – will repay you both a hundredfold.

What can I do, if I feel my child is spending too much time with the computer or television?

Only you can decide that, but many of the suggestions in the previous chapters will help; acceptance and love, with a change of some family policies, will assist certainly, but there will have to be plenty of *fun*, to make up for the lessening of electronic entertainment. Depriving children of former occupations to which they have become almost addicted requires skill and some craftiness.

An increase of parental involvement in games, outside and in, an increase in book interest through library visits and the beginnings of a read-aloud policy, if this has not been in place before: *'Hey! Listen to this!'* – a paragraph from an exciting book ... You will find ways, if you are really determined.

This book, of course, is addressed mainly to the parents of children who have not yet started school. One of its aims has been to help these parents guide their children through early childhood, so that such problems will be much less likely to arise.

The formula is simple, when you come to think of it, for the youngest *and* for school-age children: plenty of interaction with real things and people; active and imaginative play; creative activities and games; and books, books, books! Books owned and borrowed from the library, stories read aloud ... all this has been said before, but can never be said too often. Of *course* it requires adult energy and involvement! As a parent, the choice is yours.

Books for parents and children
six

We have included this section as a chapter to make sure you read it! All too often a 'bibliography' or 'book list' is overlooked or ignored.

Books for parents

We feel that this list, which we have purposely kept *short*, will help you to stay interested and involved in *your* child's learning life.

There are many experiences that children need in the preschool years to help them to become avid readers. We have not stressed books on the *teaching* of reading but rather, we have selected books which will help parents to provide experiences that their children will certainly need if they are to become good readers.

All books described are straightforward, readable and, at the time of writing, in print. This means that any good bookshop should be able to obtain them if asked. One would also expect to find most of them in libraries.

We have intentionally avoided recommending heavy, 'scholarly' books, no matter how good. Parents are busy people who are likely to be tired when they finally come to reading about their craft. We have not included publishers or prices of the books in these lists. All good libraries and bookshops will find them for you; and the Internet is a very useful tool here too.

If you have any difficulty buying or borrowing any title, ask your public library to get it in for you. Librarians are usually pleased to have borrowers use the services they provide.

Every book on this list could give you pleasure, information and, we hope, inspiration. Try them.

***Babies Need Books*, by Dorothy Butler**

This book is written for parents who enjoyed *Reading Begins at Home*. The author has listed over 400 suggested titles in this longer book, with separate chapters describing children, their characteristics and needs, from birth to six years.

***Reading Magic*, by Mem Fox**

The author's emphasis throughout is on reading aloud, and she gives a wealth of information about how, when and why. A chatty rather than academic book; good to dip into, often.

***The Reading Bug*, by Paul Jennings**

Another very readable book, by a well-known Australian author of children's books. Suggested titles for reading aloud to children of all ages are listed throughout, and there is a section entitled 'Brilliant Books' at the end. Jennings's tone is clear and humorous. Sensible, practical advice abounds in this very enjoyable book.

***Great Books to Read Aloud*, by Jacqueline Wilson**

Seventy good books, divided into three age groups from birth to 11, are brilliantly presented. The 30 '0 to 5' picture books are each given a two-page spread, with the original illustrations on both pages. Each title is described, with wide margins on each page (in bright colours) making suggestions about reading, and giving reasons for sharing. An attractive entertaining book, with excellent pointers for parents.

***The Rough Guide to Children's Books*, by Nicholas Tucker**

This is a compact little book, by an English authority, devoted entirely to children's books from birth to five. Each title is well-described, and most are illustrated. Comments on each level are included. An invaluable help for any parent.

***Rocket Your Child into Reading*, by Jackie French**

This attractive book might see any parent right through their children's growth from birth to fluent reading and writing. The chapters are well-labelled and described in the index, making it easy to find any topic: *Where to begin, Help with spelling, When to ask for help* … and so on. Especially useful for the parent whose child is having difficulties, but a really good, family reference book for anyone to keep on hand.

There are many more books available, but those listed above will provide a place to start. You can face your children's childhood with confidence and the expectation of fun. And experience proves that parental help works *only* if it can be fun, for both parties. Children need to be enjoyed if they are to become enjoying people. And surely this is what we want for them, before all else.

Books for children

The following list of books for reading aloud is intended as a guide only. Many, many suitable books are available. Library borrowing will augment home ownership, provide hints for buying, and introduce children to a very good habit.

Birth to 18 months

Cloth books used to be dull and dreary, but these days are bright and durable – ideal for a baby to suck or even, in some cases, take into the bath.

For example:

Around the Garden, **by Lucy Cousins**, and other titles in the same series, are wordless, brilliantly illustrated cloth books for babies to literally cut their teeth on.

Board books are almost as durable and should have minimal text.

Examples:

Where Does Maisy Live?, **by Lucy Cousins**, and other 'Maisy' titles.

Five Little Ducks, **by Penny Dann**, and other titles in this series, for example ***The Wheels on the Bus***.

Mrs Wishy-Washy, **by Joy Cowley**, illustrated by Elizabeth Fuller. This is a classic and should not be missed.

Other titles suitable for the youngest age-group usually have a brief repetitive text and brightly coloured pictures.

Examples:

Splash!, **by Flora McDonnell**.

Each Peach Pear Plum, **by Janet and Allan Ahlberg**.

Baby Talk, **by Judy Hindley**, illustrated by Brita Granström.

Brown Bear, Brown Bear, What Do You See?, **by Bill Martin Jnr**, illustrated by Eric Carle.

Ten, Nine, Eight, **by Molly Bang**.

Goodnight Moon, **by Margaret Wise Brown**.

A nursery rhyme collection acquired at this stage will give years of service. Choose from dozens of versions, at a wide range of prices. Your enthusiasm in using the rhymes is more important than the actual volume – but you will enjoy a beautiful book as much as your child.

Examples:

***My Very First Mother Goose*, edited by Iona Opie**, illustrated by Rosemary Wells.

***Tomie dePaola's Mother Goose*, by Tomie dePaola.**

***The Random House Book of Mother Goose*, by Arnold Lobel.**

Equally vital at this stage, and all the others, is a good collection of rhymes, jingles and action verses.

***Five Little Monkeys: Over 50 Action and Counting Rhymes*, by Zita Newcombe** is an excellent, illustrated example, though there are many others, great and small.

***Finger Rhymes*, by Marc Brown.**

18 months to three years

Children's understood vocabulary at this stage exceeds their speech by a long way, if they have been read to, talked to and sung to since birth. They are ready for simple stories, but will still relish favourites from babyhood and, of course, nursery rhymes. Repetition is appreciated.

Simple story examples:

***Hairy Maclary from Donaldson's Dairy*, by Lynley Dodd.**

***Dear Zoo*, by Rod Campbell.**

***Who Sank the Boat?*, by Pamela Allen.**

***Duck in the Truck*, by Jez Alborough.**

***Mr Gumpy's Outing*, by John Burningham.**

***My Cat Likes to Hide in Boxes*, by Eve Sutton**, illustrated by Lynley Dodd.

***Peepo!*, by Janet and Alan Ahlberg.**

***The Very Hungry Caterpillar*, by Eric Carle.**

***Dig, Dig, Digging*, by Margaret Mayo**, illustrated by Alex Ayliffe.

***The Owl and the Pussycat*, by Edward Lear.**

Whose Ears? (and other titles), **by Jeanette Rowe.**

Duckie's Rainbow (and other titles), **by Frances Barry.**

***Fancy That!*, by Pamela Allen.**

***Out of the Egg*, by Tina Matthews.**

***Alfie Gets in First*, by Shirley Hughes**, and other 'Alfie' titles.

***The Snowy Day*, by Ezra Jack Keats**, and other titles.

Approaching three years is a good time to start looking for a suitable collection of the more simple traditional stories (*The Gingerbread Man*, *The Little Red Hen*, and so on etc). The following excel in this field:

The Orchard Book of Nursery Stories, **by Sophie Windham**.

The Helen Oxenbury Nursery Collection is a useful collection containing nursery rhymes and nursery stories. Beautifully illustrated by this noted artist.

Paul Galdone's individual titles (***The Gingerbread Boy***, ***The Three Billy Goats Gruff***, and others) are ideal, from about two and a half years.

Three to five years

A very wide range of subjects, and considerable complexity, will be appreciated by the book-wise three to fives, as well as old 'baby' favourites (especially when over-tired or unwell). Many two-and-a-halfs will also enjoy books from this list; but it is wise not to push. Some children like to listen to the same title over and over again – often a very simple, repetitive book which means something to them alone. (We know of a small boy's addiction to Dr Seuss's *Green Eggs and Ham* which threatened to drive his father mad!)

Here we go then. We have listed the titles in a very general easiest-to-hardest order. And remember: these are just a very few of the many fine books available.

A Lion in the Meadow, **by Margaret Mahy**, illustrated by Jenny Williams.

The Tiger Who Came to Tea, **by Judith Kerr**.

The Elephant and the Bad Baby, **by Elfrida Vipont**, illustrated by Raymond Briggs.

The Little Yellow Digger (and other 'Digger' titles), **by Betty Gilderdale**, illustrated by Alan Gilderdale.

The Potato People, **by Pamela Allen**.

The Tale of Peter Rabbit and ***The Tale of Benjamin Bunny***, **by Beatrix Potter**.

The Gruffalo, **by Julia Donaldson**, illustrated by Axel Scheffler.

We're Going on a Bear Hunt, **by Michael Rosen**, illustrated by Helen Oxenbury.

The Lighthouse Keeper's Lunch (and other 'Lighthouse' titles), **by Ronda and David Armitage**.

A Summery Saturday Morning (and other Mahy titles), **by Margaret Mahy**, illustrated by Selina Young.

The Christmas Caravan, **by Jennifer Beck**, illustrated by Robyn Belton.

Where the Wild Things Are, **by Maurice Sendak**.

Dogger, **by Shirley Hughes**.

The Big Concrete Lorry, **by Shirley Hughes**, and other titles in the ***Tales of Trotter Street*** series.

Dazzling Diggers and other titles (e.g. ***Amazing Aeroplanes***), **by Tony Mitton and Ant Parker**.

Chameleon, Chameleon, **by Joy Cowley**, photographs by Nic Bishop.

Grandpa's Slippers (and other titles), **by Joy Watson**, illustrated by Wendy Hodder.

Mike Mulligan and his Steam Shovel, **by Virginia Lee Burton**.

The ***Curious George*** series, **by Margret Rey and H.A. Rey**.

Blueberries for Sal, **by Robert McCloskey**.

Corduroy, **by Don Freeman**.

The Cow Who Fell in the Canal, **by Phyllis Krasilovsky**.

Between four and five years is an ideal time to start regularly reading aloud from a 'non-picture book'. Such stories help children to develop their listening skills and use their imaginations. 'Making pictures in your head' is what the mature reader must do. Providing an early start on this skill is an excellent idea. Note: This practice should be 'as well as', not 'instead of', picture book sharing!

Many of the best books are still the old ones in this category. Very young children do not change from generation to generation. Their concerns remain the same; and a good story is a good story!

Suggested titles:

Pooh Bear (and ***The House at Pooh Corner*** as the child grows), **by A.A. Milne**.

The Puffin Book of Stories for Five-Year-Olds, edited by Wendy Cooling, illustrated by Steve Fox.

Milly-Molly-Mandy Stories (and other titles), **by Joyce Lankester Brisley**.

Teddy Robinson (and other titles), **by Joan G. Robinson**.

And a few poetry collections:

When We Were Very Young (and ***Now We Are Six*** as your child gets older), **by A.A. Milne**.

The Usborne Book of Poems for Little Children, collected by Sam Taplin, illustrated by Masumi Furukawa.

Note: Poetry collections for the very young are hard to find, but rhyme and jingle books will continue to be popular.

You will become the best judge of what *your* child likes, and frequent read-aloud sessions are the best possible way to ensure a close relationship between you both, and set your young son or daughter on the road to reading.

Good luck, and good reading!

Use these two pages to note down titles of books that your child enjoys:

Title	Author	Child's reaction

Title	Author	Child's reaction